FOR
HERE'S HOPIN
THIS ONE
MOVES YOU
AS I WAS MOVED
TO WRITE IT &
PUT IT TOGETHER...

Made in America

SOME TALL
TRUTHFUL
TALES
OF OUR
SOCIO/POLITICAL TIMES
&
THE STORY OF
MY WIFE & KIDS
&
ONE ABOUT
YOUR OLD MAN
AND ME
AND CAPITANO NORB'S
OLD DOG —

LOVE, ZEEEE

ALSO BY ROBERT M. ZOSCHKE

Door County Blues

Reflections Upon the 50th Anniversary of Jack Kerouac's On the Road (Co-Editor and Contributing Writer)

Made in America

Robert M. Zoschke

Street Corner Press
corner of Armitage & Clybourn
Chicago, Illinois 60614

Street Corner Press

Chicago, Illinois, USA

Made in America

by Robert M. Zoschke

FIRST EDITION, FIRST PRINTING, JUNE 2010

Front Cover Art: "Poets on the Road in a Ford Truck."
Photograph of Joie Powell by Robert M. Zoschke. Originally
published by THE MOON—The Publication of Writing and Art.

Back Cover Art: "Twenty Twins Toes" photo by Robert M. Zoschke.

Layout by Robert M. Zoschke

Graphic Art & Production Design by Sarah Elizabeth Burkey

ISBN: 978-0-578-06037-8

PRINTED IN THE UNITED STATES OF AMERICA

the author & his wife Joie in the early days

*This book is dedicated
to the memory of Peter Nicoli,
an indelible American original.*

*And to Peter's son, Steve,
the closest to a genetic brother
I could ever have.*

*And to Joie Powell—
the finest woman
I never thought I would ever find.*

Table of Contents

1   Bored on the Fourth of July, 2008
5   Global Warning
6   American Spirit
7   Woman and Man
8   Solitaire
9   Normal…
10   Hey Ma
11   survival of the fittest
12   new economy of scale
13   stiff upper lip
15   just another normal human being
17   a dog of a poem
24   when the pen is the needle and the paper is the spoon
28   forever sordid shame
31   Bipartisan
33   the swords are in little hands
40   photos by Joie Powell and Robert M. Zoschke
70   Elegy for The Pistol
76   only the serious know
78   only your hands tremble
82   Ides of March sarong
84   Front Porch Blues
86   the yearning
88   Listen…
89   Need the Rain?
91    $9.84 an hour
94   are you a…
98   The Sit-Down
101   What Matters Most
108   Circle of Life
110   The Lesson
114   poems in her head

Author's Acknowledgement
About the Author

"I'd rather be writing love poems."

—Lawrence Ferlinghetti—

"Your mother and I went to Walmart today. Everything I looked at was made in China, made in China, made in China, made wherever the hell else. Nothin' was made in America anymore. And people wonder why our economy is in the crapper?"

—Robert D. Zoschke—

Bored on the Fourth of July, 2008

along the tattered shoreline
of the diminishing and tainted
once great Lake Michigan

I light a red Marlboro
with a God Bless The USA
disposable lighter made in China

by Asian child slaves
the latest whoreflesh
replacing NAFTA poisoned Mexicans

email spam from Racing USA
offers foreign made slave labor treats
Low Priced Patriotic NASCAR shirts

AOL News of The Day blurb
flashes me today's question
are you a Patriot?

AOL News of The Day blurb
prods me to reconsider and vote
in the Daily Hot Seat Poll

I don't need
to reconsider
jack shit

far too many USA young boys
getting dragged through
Union Busting Walmarts

want Single Parent Momma
to buy them the latest and greatest
Grand Theft Auto video game

far too many USA young boys
following Momma to the
Licensed Drug Cartel pharmacy counter

for the ever so all important re-up
on the Ritalin prescription
and an afterthought box of Fred Flintstone vitamins

supposedly I could make all this shit float away
with the latest new wonder pill advertised on
The National Broadcasting Corporation Channel

unless I wound up a God Bless The USA
Fine Print Warning Side Effects Victim
with hives or paranoid sweats or anal leakage

I want John McCain to stop calling
every campaign crowd
His Friends

I want Barack Obama to start explaining
what he would actually say
to all the Hostile Enemy Leaders

I want Hillary Clinton to start detailing
how the hell she managed to find eleven million
personal dollars to infuse into her campaign

I want Bill Clinton to explain how much of his
hundred million in '07 earnings actually came from
the scumbags he pardoned before he left the White House

I want Commander in Miniature Bushie
to cover up the flag pin on his lapel
with his cheerleader blow horn from his Yale Daze

I want Dickless Cheney
to spend some time at the shooting range
before he goes hunting again

I want Lou Dobbs and Bill O'Reilly
to quit bitching about illegal aliens
and start mowing their own lawns

I want the Tree Hugger Organizations
and the Card Carrying PETA Swines
to spend all their money on homeless shelters

I want a gallon of gasoline .
to cost less than
a gallon of milk

I want every Middle School in our Nation
to pause on the class trips to Washington D.C.
and try a trip to City Lights Bookstore

I want to see grade school kids
serving at street corner lemonade stands
instead of stealing music onto their I-Pods

I want to see the Federal Reserve
stop rewarding Ivy League firms with bailout prizes
that just about cover their annual executive bonuses

I want to see everyone with a Lobbyist business card
kept against their will at Walter Reed hospital
until the rats chew off their lobbying feet

Am I a Patriot?
You're Goddamn
Right I Am

Bored
on the
Fourth of July

Global Warning

so let's see if I got this right
all of us countries with nuclear bombs
are telling countries without nuclear bombs
they can't have any nuclear bombs
as if the Indians with all the land
told the white men without any land
they couldn't have any land at all
oh that's right the Indians never said that
the Indians didn't have
the heavy artillery

American Spirit

even when it was
John Wayne
I always rooted for
the Indians
in the Cowboy movies

Woman and Man

a woman finds
anger
easier and better
than stress

a man finds
resentment
easier and better
than anger

a woman with
a real point to make
bends the truth
to make her point

a man with
a point to make
bends the truth
to hide his real point

such is the cause of
too many shake ups
too many break ups
not enough wake ups

or maybe
this is just
a man's
point of view

Solitaire

waiting for others
to do things differently
is more lonely
than solitaire
with an old deck
of ruffled cards

Normal...

...is just a cycle
on a washing machine

Hey Ma

she asked for
cigarettes
cell phone minutes
and cherry Rolaids
and that is just
what her mother bought her

survival of the fittest

the great lake's alewife population
is decimated by foreign invasive species
such as zebra mussels and gobies
and now the seagulls can't find enough food
so the seagulls hover in a cherry orchard
feasting on cherries
as the cherry farmer
levels his shotgun and says
best not to kill as many as you can
he says it sends a better message to clip just one
then a seagull cries out while fluttering its only wing

new economy of scale

corporate lifer
pension plan recipient
401k participant
moving up the ladder
moving for the company
relocation benefits package
perks perks perks
even somebody to read
the fine print on the new mortgage
and explain it all in one easy phone call

corporate books cooked
pension plan insolvency
401k evaporation
adjustable rate mortgage kicks in
bent over by the company
no courtesy of a reach around
perks perks perks
now a free meal after every shift
of asking *do you want to make that*
a combo instead of just the sandwich?

stiff upper lip

no money in my pockets
none
just a cup holder full of change
in my truck's floorboard console

I needed something to make me
feel
not so fuckless bad
so I conjured some bullshit for the bank teller

my cup holder can't even hold a
coffee
on account of all this change
that's what I was going to tell her

then I remembered my old neighborhood
uncle
how all the hens in our tribe always praised Tony
for never failing to keep a stiff upper lip

back in the old neighborhood things were
different
rotary phones televisions with pliers for busted knobs
old wives tales told with broken grammar

nobody knew how to express what Uncle Tony really
had
a built in always working bullshit detector
and the balls to always use it on himself

so I walked into the bank and scattered my
change
told the teller hey I'm sorry I'd feel worse
plunking all this down at the grocery store

I walked out with twelve dollars and thirteen unlucky
cents
then drove past the grocery store to the post office
for stamps to send poems out into the wilderness

just another normal human being

I remember back when I was a kid
on vacation with my friend Jim
at his grandparents' house out east

my friend's gramma had an invalid husband
and she had spent her whole married life
devoted to caring for him

after he died she got to talking
about being overweight and
whether she would lose the weight

she talked about the times he would carp at her
how stressed out it would make her feel
how it made her think about ice cream in the freezer

she said there were times when she would
finally get him settled into bed then
she would go straight for the ice cream

and now I remember her saying that
after a heated stew with my lover woman
has me seeing a pack of cigarettes in my head

sure I could go buy a pack and start smoking again
but I have that vision of my friend's gramma
stressed out and tearing into the ice cream

she was an incredibly fine lady
and her husband was an incredibly fine man
they were just normal human beings

dealing with
the shit stirred up
by life's storm

no ice cream in the freezer
no cigarette in my hand
maybe I am just another normal human being

a dog of a poem

in memory of Shadow Blei

she only gets this way with you
Jude said with a touch of exasperation
one afternoon
after I appeared in the driveway
and Shadow bounded over
recognizing my truck
before it neared and stopped
and Shadow started going berserk
as I cooed to her in my
just for Shadow falsetto
in a tone of voice
soft enough
for Jude to maybe not catch on
yet loud enough
for Shadow to want to hear it
higher and louder
the way I would coo to her
when I pulled in the driveway
and got out of the truck
with nobody
but Shadow and me around

she always gets this way with me
I told Jude
as I thought about the times
it was only Shadow and me around
like the first time I ever reached
into a box of smoked salmon
on the passenger seat of the truck
bringing out a chunk
that made Shadow lick her lips
sweeter than a human being ever has
then I climbed out of the truck
Shadow prancing and whining loudly
as I kept cooing
Shadow…Shadow…Shadow…
while making sure the first piece
I offered her
had no bones in it
then Shadow got my hand
along with that first piece of salmon
then Shadow learned
in that forever after dog way
to take each piece on her tongue
as preciously
as a woman
letting an engagement ring
that she really wants
slip onto her finger
and that's how Shadow
took all the other pieces of salmon
though like a good dog
and a good Bohunk from the old neighborhood
Shadow liked a hunk of skin best of all

all of that in my mind's eye
as Jude said
Norb's in the coop
so off I headed
Jude trailing off
Shadow following me
as Shadow had
on other occasions
when I didn't have salmon but
Norb's car was in the driveway
and I would finish cooing to Shadow
by saying let's go see Papa

visits in the coop with Norb
during which Shadow
would sit right outside the door
like she did during the visit
when I told Norb
I gotta go take a leak
and went outside the coop
and Shadow started her hyper whine
which led to Shadow
finally calming down
when I started cooing to her
in a soft low voice
Shadow…Shadow…Shadow…
which made her relax and sit down
with her massive hind quarters
pressed against the back of my legs
as the forest's fallen leaves
crinkled until I was through

yes after that first driveway encounter
spent removing salmon bones
and feeding Shadow
I never could pull into that driveway
without Shadow
damn near climbing inside my truck
while the door was open
and I got my seat belt untangled
though I must admit
I brought it upon myself
the second time
I pulled in with smoked salmon
and rolled the window down
cooing Shadow…Shadow…Shadow…
upon which it didn't take long
for her to catch a whiff
of the smoked salmon in the passenger's seat
and rear up on her German Shepherd legs
like an anxious Kentucky Stallion
so every time I pulled in after that
Shadow damn near climbed into the truck
because Shadow knew
in the way a good dog knows
even if her nose wasn't smelling it
it didn't hurt to look just in case

one writer with a dog nearby
alone in his coop
one writer with enough
good published work to fill a coop
so as to displace and do away with
the rejection slips never forgotten
that had to be tolerated
to fill the coop's shelves
one writer with enough
awards and
notification letters of awards
to place strategically
out of sight in the coop
where the rejection slips
never forgotten
used to be

one writer with a dog nearby
his coop where war was waged
one writer with a dog nearby
after winning the war
that simply had to be fought
with his life
the war of toleration
with all those literary establishments
that decades gone by
had often told him
what he sent them
were dogs
without ever often enough
taking the time
to write a letter that said
they were good dogs

one writer with a dog nearby
a dog always to be counted on
to tell the writer
like only a dog can
that the writer was right
for waging the war
with his life
one writer with a dog nearby
after too many times
when it was only the dog nearby
that knew how to help the writer realize
he actually was right
and he actually had won

one writer with a dog nearby
tolerating another writer's visits
until reaching the point
of looking forward to those visits
simply for the reason
that another writer had come to town
and stuck around
fighting the same war
rejection slip by rejection slip
with just enough goddamn goofy
nonsensical sense
to find solace however he could
even if it meant
cooing to the other writer's dog

one writer with a dog nearby
dead on the porch
calling the other writer with a dog far away
but the call goes unanswered
and one writer has to figure out
how to hoist the dead dog
without the other writer
who knows the war of it

which probably explains
why so many writers
have always had dogs
and maybe this is just
a dog of a poem
or maybe not
only the Shadow knows
maybe the Coyote too

when the pen is the needle
and the paper is the spoon

for Dave Church, Rest in Peace

today
the mail box
offered nothing
of merit

so
I'm reading again
the postcards and letters
from Dave Church

one
of the few proud true poets
that not enough people
have ever read

today
the mail box
offered another
goddamn reason

why
the few proud true poets
like Dave Church
aren't heard and read enough

glossy
promotional mailer
from what used to be
a proud true underground bookstore

WORKSHOP
the promo mailer hollers
VERBAL ROUNDABOUTS
WRITING WITH OBSESSIVE VOCABULARIES

the
workshop teacher
has a promo blurb that reeks of
rotgut academician flatulence

assistant
professor of English
teaching courses in
American poetry and creative writing

with
an MFA in poetry
and a PhD in
comparative literature

plus
this professor published a chapbook
once
back in 2001

whoever
suffers through that godforsaken
three hour workshop
would get more ideas worth writing about

if
they blew off the workshop
and rode around Milwaukee in a cab
bullshitting for three hours with the cabbie

though
they wouldn't be so lucky
to have a cabbie
like Dave Church was

it
was his hack job
driving that cab around
and Hack Job was the title of one of his books

that
hack job paid for Dave's
pens and paper and postage and electricity for his typer
and some other not so important things

Dave
and I always wound up talking on the phone
when one of us was in the laugh instead of cry mode
and one of us called and laugh we did

because
we knew what writers know
we knew when to go for the laugh instead of the cry
when the pen is the needle and the paper is the spoon

when
the only thing felt inside
to cast merit out into the world
meets more rejection slips than acceptance letters

when
someone with enough money to get a PhD
and enough desire to write one chapbook in eleven years
teaches workshops to folks who might want to be writers

the
masterpiece that Dave Church was working on
through eleven hack job years of cab driving
in addition to all his writing

was
a collected anthology
with a working title of
Alternative Voices in American Poetry since 1950

you
can bet your bottom dollar
the Verbal Roundabout Academician soon to
soil the bookstore stage isn't in there

forever sordid shame

Michael Jackson
finally crumbled and gave way
underneath the
inescapable weight
of his
forever sordid shame

in New York City
his oblivious fans gather in mass
outside the Apollo
as the internet shows us
his oblivious fans around the world
crying as they cradle his CDs

New Millennium
ignorant tears for Michael Jackson
cascading like a virus
cascading like his
misanointed fame
and misspent fortune

nobody from his early inner circle
nobody from his equally scarred family
finding the guts to speak
about his forever sordid shame
so that tears
of truth could flow

the hollow shallow rapture of the lemmings
and the perverse gluttony of the CD listening suckerfish
fuels the internet blogs and news reports
until all that remains to be done
is for the New York Times
to shake its Thesaurus over his death

except
that is not really all
that remains
in need
of really
being done

long after the
pop music serenade
of Michael Jackson's music
fades into silence with the passing of time
and the passing of generations
an eerier silence will remain

the eerie silence
too often common
in the inner circle families
where children are
bludgeoned with
dysfunction and abuse

the dysfunction and abuse
scarred Michael Jackson forever
trapped him in a noxious cocoon
that he could not escape from
no matter how many body altering plastic surgeries
and mind numbing shots of dope

the dysfunction and abuse
that left him embodying
the all too often
sadistic classic symptom
of the abused becoming
the abuser

how many millions of dollars
raked in by Michael Jackson's
hollow shallow lunacy of fame
were paid out to the little boys who started to talk
and how many millions were spent
on the theme parks that ensnared the little boys?

right now in the streets of Iran
a morbidly megalomaniac dictator
has snipers on his palace rooftops
mowing down his own people
who want nothing more than freedom
from having to dress their women like beekeepers

right now in the streets of America
an abused abuser
who couldn't scalpel away
or bleach away or dope away
his forever sordid shame
draws the wrong kind of tears

Bipartisan

the rest of the world
is filled with
growing economies that make things
and answer America's
customer service calls

Treasury Secretary Paulson
gave billions to U.S. banks
so they could use it to buy banks in China
so China can afford to
keep buying U.S. treasury bonds

President Clinton makes millions of U.S. dollars
from speaking in foreign countries
that make things we used to make
before Clinton championed NAFTA
to ensure we don't make things

President Bushie took his millions of
oil dollars and bought a Texas mansion
with a foreign made wide screen television
still not showing American soldier caskets
coming home from foreign lands

the misfit mongrels of patronage
otherwise known as the House and Senate
gather themselves to complain about
President Obama wanting billions
for government jobs to guarantee American Work

Welcome to the New World Order
modern american style
please follow the New U.S. Road Map
just bend over spread your cheeks and
don't expect the courtesy of a reach around

but please remember to tell your sons and daughters
they can still get automatic no cost
after waiting in the long line
health care benefits
if they sign up for New Duty in Afghanistan

the place where our sons and daughters
can serve our
New World Order Homeland
by playing hopscotch
with NATO forces

going village to village
burning opium poppy fields
of only those tribal warlords
that don't pay the graft
of growing opium poppy

if you don't understand by now
good luck to you in trying to figure out why
so many sons and daughters in Our Homeland
are busy stealing prescription pills
and Heroin is the New Comeback King

the swords are in little hands

once upon a time
I spent one decade
too many
as a willing pawn
checkmated
in a king's game of fool's gold

along the way
I found hospital beds
bone graft
hip replacement
staph infection
blood clots and pulmonary embolism

along the way
lawyers found me
their triple seven slot machine
eyes
promised vengeance
for a cut of the take

I knew I had to
shun the lawyers
and disavow vengeance
if I wanted to heal
but I was still a disciple
of that rigged chessboard

along the way
still living for serving the kings
awash in their money and headed toward dying
I found more hospital beds
more blood clots
a couple strokes

a stammered tongue
a staggered gate
a scorched brain
I finally started realizing
the fool's gold kings had little hands
and I was tired of being a pawn

I left cities behind
and moved to the woods
where my writing made me
a few friends who helped me heal
where my writing made me
the enemy of fool's gold kings wanting pawns

I have seen people from coast to coast
anoint themselves with fool's gold
and now they are in new millennium bankruptcy
without ever listening to a Dylan album
but now they know
money doesn't talk it swears

I have seen bookstore owners
full of light and love
for reading and writing
absolutely devoting their lives
to keeping their stores
open for business

I have seen fearful loathing
trust fund babies
become bookstore owners
without loving reading or writing
they smile at the morning mirror
brushing their teeth with little hands

and as the famous playwright said
a funny thing happened on the way to the forum
one of those Freewheelin' Bob Dylan
simple twists of fate
made me an editor
on an international book project

that book born
out of light and love
took me
across the country
and across the ocean
through dueling swords

along the way
a splendid poet
from the New York Times front page
took to a stage and
read his work in that book
and he called it an important book

along the way
a splendid poet
from Naropa University
never even bothered
to say thanks
for contributor copies

along the way
a splendid poet
in the American Academy of Arts and Letters
who designed the front cover of that book
declared the book
a stunner

along the way
a splendid writer
one of Ken Kesey's Merry Pranksters
never even bothered
to say thanks
for contributor copies

along the way
a splendid writer
still in high school and never before published
never even bothered
to say thanks
for contributor copies

along the way
a famous television actor
without any prior poetic publication
never even bothered
to say thanks
for contributor copies

along the way
a famous Hollywood movie star
who's a splendid award winning poet
wrote by hand with thanks and praise
upon seeing his work
in that book

along the way
a splendid poet
in the small press all his life
read from that book on stage
then handed me one of his own books
a PEN Award winning book he signed *with love*

and I do not know
if all of that meant
I was a good editor
or a bad editor
but it reminded me
the swords are in little hands

then I came back
to insular small town life
deep in the rural woods
where the fool's gold kings
shape pawns for themselves
with their little hands

I saw the same
big city
dueling swords
in the small town woods
but by then I was certain
of the tools of my trade

light and love and pen to paper
and fingers to the typer
I kept writing
hell bent to show
the little hands
what big hands could do

and a book called Door County Blues was born
a book for the people in those woods
the people not wanting to be pawns
the people fighting swords with big hands
and the people wanting to be pawns
the people swinging swords with little hands

and then
a whole boat load
of funny things
happened
on the way
to the forum

the people
not wanting to be pawns
smiled and said
it felt cool to be in that book
they said hey thanks
for writing about us

the people
fighting swords with big hands
stopped me at the grocery store
and bought me drinks in the taverns
and told me they never thought
somebody would write such truths

one of them even took a picture of herself
reading my book
and put it on her MySpace page
and best of all
she's the finest most courageous
woman I have ever known

the people
wanting to be pawns
cowered and shuddered and looked away
when I passed them on the street
they stared into their drinks when I entered a tavern
they kept forgetting my name when I said hello to them

the people
swinging swords with little hands
purchased radio ads touting
their newspaper as the cure for my book
and they made sure my name didn't appear
in the newspaper event listings when I had book signings

that newspaper
being produced with little hands
kept on running their radio ads
knocking my book
but it did not stop my book from becoming
a number one bestseller listed in that paper's rankings

and I do not know
if all of that meant
I wrote a good book or a bad book
but it proved to me that every now and then
the pen is mightier than the sword
and the swords are in little hands

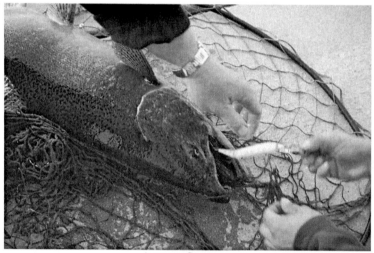

Autumn Sunset—
catching salmon from the piers in Door County, Wisconsin.

Poets on the Pier—
the author's wife, Joie, with a dandy midnight salmon.

Joie with another midnight salmon caught from the town pier in
Fish Creek, Wisconsin.

Author Rob with his stepson Kenny
and another autumn salmon caught from shore.

44

Author Rob and a fine Door County smallmouth bass.

Author Rob's stepdaughter Rachael.
Like her mother, Rachael is a mighty fine angler.

Author Rob somehow holding the camera steady while trembling over falling in love on a fishing pier in Door County, Wisconsin.

Author Rob chasing spring brown trout and battling Mother Nature.

Did you hear the one about the Sox Fan and the Cubs Fan that went
fishing together? Author Rob and his godson Timmy at Water's End in
Door County.

Poets Stuck in Traffic—Author Rob at the wheel, Joie with the camera, and Rachael writing poems in her head.

Sweet Home Chicago—Author Rob trying to convince Kenny that Michael Jordan only stuck his tongue out on the basketball court.

Poets Almost There—Author Rob and Kenny, on the road with Joie and Rachael, long gone from Wisconsin and nearing Florida.

Poets Dressed to the Nines—
Author Rob and Joie ready for a night on the town.

TWINS! Author Rob and Joie on the day of her shower.

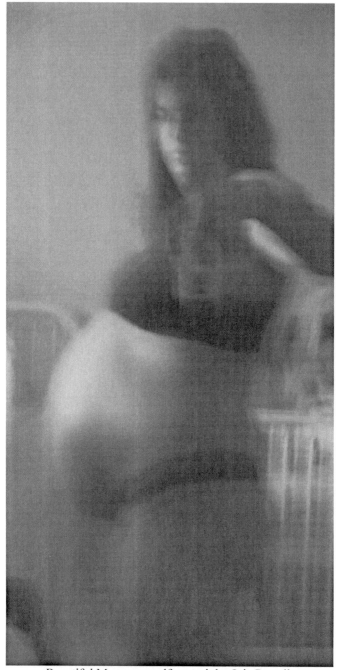

Beautiful Momma—self portrait by Joie Powell.

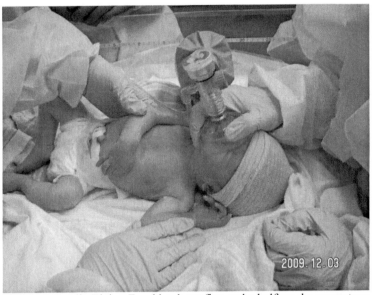

"Baby A" Amelia Elaine Zoschke, born five and a half weeks premature.

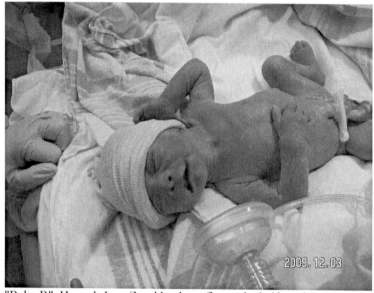

"Baby B" Hannah Jane Zoschke, born five and a half weeks premature.

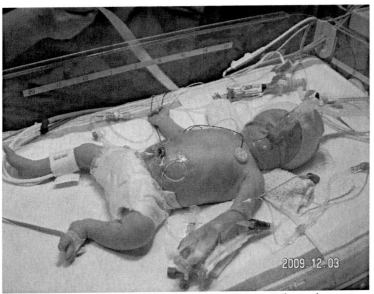

Amelia at the Neo Natal ICU in Green Bay, Wisconsin.

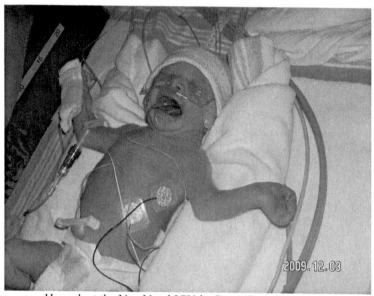

Hannah at the Neo Natal ICU in Green Bay, Wisconsin.

Proud Parents—Author Rob and Joie with Amelia and Hannah at the
Neo Natal ICU in Green Bay.

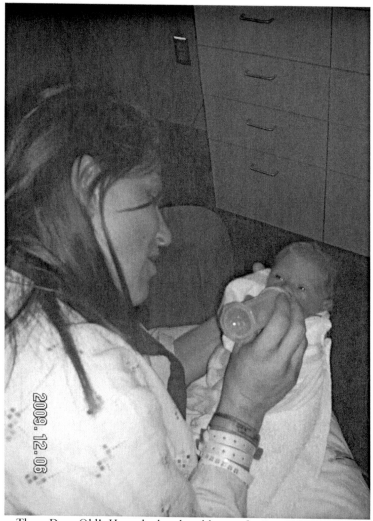

Three Days Old! Hannah already with eyes for Beautiful Momma.

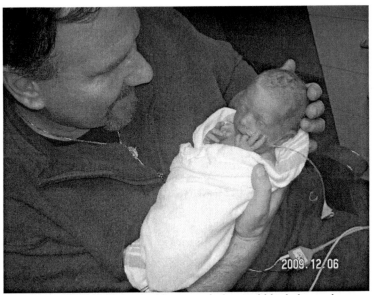

Author Rob realizing just how much the world had changed...
Three-days-old Hannah asleep in Daddy's arms.

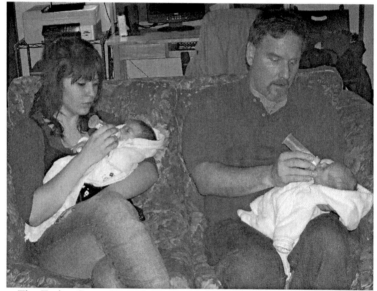

The Twins Come Home! Rachael with her sisters, and Author Rob trying to do as well as Rachael.

Nana Grandma Zoschke with Amelia Elaine.

Grandpa Bob Zoschke, first time holding Amelia.

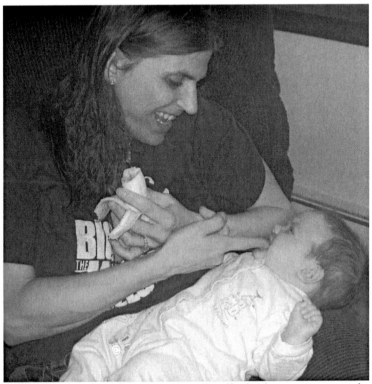

Beautiful Momma trying to convince Amelia that bananas taste good.

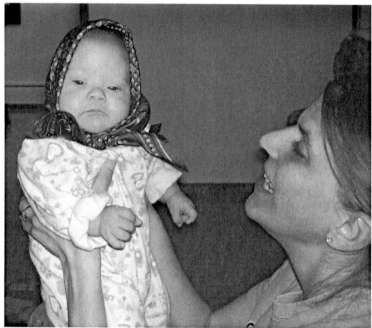

Hannah pays tribute to her roots—wearing her babushka like an old neighborhood Czech girl on the South Side of Chi Town.

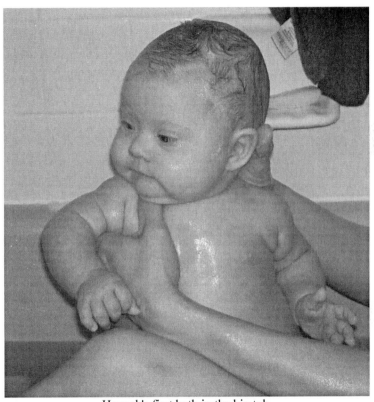

Hannah's first bath in the big tub.

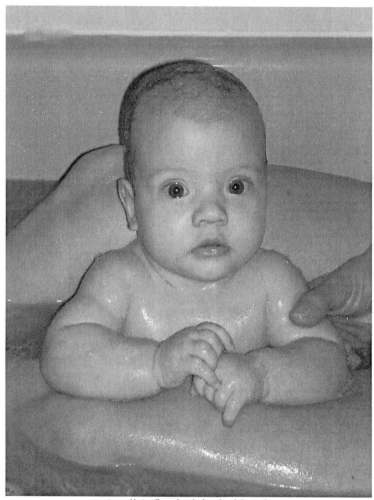

Amelia's first bath in the big tub.

On the Road Again—taking the twins downtown in Chi Town.

Elegy for The Pistol

my friend Steve and I
had a nickname for his father
we called him The Pistol

it came natural to us
calling his father The Pistol
it was a nickname that fit

based on the old neighborhood
unspoken definition of
the guy who was The Pistol

in the old neighborhood
there was only one guy
worthy of being called The Pistol

hardly ever was one guy
a cool dude and a hot shit and the one
to speak up when something had to be said
the one to stay quiet when silence was golden
the one everybody listened to no matter what
the one who always watched your back
the one to never pull a fast one on
the one to always want on your side
the one to never ever fuck with
the one to go see if someone fucked with you

not to mention
the one
who could go

from heartfelt seriousness
to heartfelt humor
in the blink of an eye

and never miss a beat in the conversation
no matter if he was stone cold sober
or halfway through cocktail number ten

and Holy Christ yes
that's a helluva lot
to say about one man

there was always so much stuff
going on in the old neighborhood
such as trying to find out if a morning
line ten to one shot really could
steal the first half of the daily double
going wire to wire like Go For Gin
so a guy like Peter
the guy with
the most credentials
he was The Pistol

he sounded tough and strong
yet full of tender heart like always
searching for and finding
the humor vein
tapping it like a gold miner
the last few times we talked
on the telephone
before the cancer
went all the way
and he was gone

when Steve called me with the news
Steve sounded tough and strong
yet full of tender heart like always
he sounded like his father
and he did a better job
of holding back the tears
than I did after hanging up
and walking out into a moonless night
thinking about something Peter taught me
once upon a time in the old neighborhood

there was a wedding in Boston
Steve and I were both invited to
we were staying at his family's house
the house where Steve was raised
in an Italian enclave outside of Boston

Steve got hung up in Chi Town
I flew into Boston a day early
and off I went to the old neighborhood
feasting at the kitchen table
on Gramma Nicoli's side of the house

it was getting on toward evening
Steve's mother was still at work
Steve's sister was still at work
his father wasn't home and Gramma said
just go on down wait for him at the club

down where? I asked her
down at the club she said
where's the club? I wondered out loud
down at the end of the driveway she said
so off I went…

it looked like another house in the neighborhood
when I drove in from the airport
but once I got inside there was no doubt
it was an Italian Social Club
and I had some explaining to do

I walked up to the bartender and said
I'm here waiting for Peter Nicoli
and right then the dice game stopped
the card game stopped the dart game stopped
and the barkeep said *who the hell are you?*

once I got it explained who I was
they all hollered out *oh yeah sure, right*
like the chorus to a beautiful song
then all the games and the bets on the games resumed
and they all wanted to buy me a drink

when Peter finally showed up
they all lined up wanting to buy him drinks
which made sense they were mostly union guys
laborers all their lives and all of their lives
made better by Peter their union Vice President

by the time many hours had passed
through which Peter and I had talked
non stop about every kind of thing
mainly his life and my life and Life
the crowd had withered and it was time for home

I had been drinking ginger ale all night
Peter had been drinking vodka and cokes
we started up the incline of the driveway
it's easier goin' down for Christ sake Peter said
and we laughed as he leaned his arm on my shoulder

half-way up the driveway I said
I had a helluva time tonight
Peter said *Holy Christ you fit right in*
and then he took his arm from my shoulder
and raised his hand and ruffled my hair

almost all the way up the driveway
Peter hesitated then stopped in his tracks
I thought about all those vodka and cokes
how those guys had damn near wrestled over
buying one after the other for Peter

but all of a sudden Peter stood firm and tall
he looked at me with stone cold sober eyes
he put an unwavering hand on my shoulder
and then he said *you could be Italian
you could be my son*

I think of that night so often now
ever since Peter passed away
and I realize what that night taught me
how I carried with me into my life
what I learned in those words from Peter

the world would be a much better place
if every man out in the street
had the willingness inside his heart
to treat another man's son
as if he were his own son

If I hadn't learned that from Peter
I might have come up a bit short
coaching a bunch of ten year old kids
who had never skated
to a roller hockey championship

If I hadn't learned that from Peter
I might not have had back to back to back
store manager of the year awards
from Sears when it was still Sears
before Kmart bought Sears and ruined it

and the damn strangest thing of all
I realize when I think about it
is that I would still be working for Sears
if we ever had a union
and Peter was our Vice President

only the serious know

I got canned from the job that was
paying for my food and gas
and paper and ink cartridges

I was a front desk clerk at a ritzy resort
when tourist season ended there was
lots of downtime for writing on the job

if you're serious about writing
but haven't peddled a novel to New York yet
then you know what your real job is

I had to keep writing and
just before tourist season they canned me
only the serious know to call it a draw

now winter is here again
my unemployment checks are ending
I've got thirty two bucks in a bank account

my agent in NYC is backed up on his reading
he's sitting on the novel I started at that front desk
only the serious know to call it a draw

writing alone in a cold shack in the woods
my woman is ticked at me in her warm house
if you love your woman you know how serious that is

the phone rings I hope for a moment
but I know it isn't my woman
calling to make peace

an old man with a cigarette stained southern voice
doesn't say hello instead he barks *why in the hell
are you stayin in the freezin woods a Wisconsin?*

I bark *well who the hell is asking?*
while wondering if he's a bill collector
and wondering about my ticked off woman

the old man pauses
I hear him cough then he says
this is Harry Crews

Harry says *hold on
I gotta light a cigarette*
then he coughs like holy hell

Harry barks *man I gotta finish
this novel I'm workin' on
gonna be my last one my time's comin*

I don't know what to say to Harry Crews
I'm serious about my woman I love
I'm serious about my writing

Harry says *listen man I got a shack out back
it's warm down here sunny down here
we're scribblers so you know the drill by now*

Harry says *come on down man
I work inside you work out back in the shack
we'll talk about books and writers the rest of the time*

I'm 43 and I have a woman
Harry is 75 and he doesn't have a woman
only the serious know what this poem really means

only your hands tremble

for three long lonely nights
you made good use
of the loneliness
banging away
at the typer

the sky was that wicked
almost clear midnight blue
that comes a lot
during northeastern
Wisconsin winters

you kept the blinds
open as a lover's arms
and watched the murky
midnight blue sky
through the window over the typer

twelve hours straight
is a fucking cakewalk
you've been chucking around
the weights at the gym
banging the typer you feel the rush

the rush
is the solution
to your problems
and the cause
of your woman's problems

your woman has
what's considered a real job
by everybody in the world
who doesn't bang a typer
and fix what comes out

the only time
you stepped outside
during three long typer nights
was to drive the truck
into the garage

the fourth day's twelve hour shift
gives way
to the fourth night alone
and a midnight black winter sky
and it's twelve below zero outside

your woman is sleeping alone at her place
so you put on your heavy jacket
you walk outside your place
you think it's not so bad
there's no wind at all

it's too cold for any company
no animals are stirring in the woods
but the stars are out
your typer zapped neck cracks
as you look up at the stars

some crazy bastard
built a house
full of decadent
dysfunctional opulence
across the street from your place

the crazy bastard
landscaped his yard
with towering elm trees
so you cannot clearly see
a rare blood orange moon

you stay outside
for a long while
you think it's not that bad
no wind at all
and you know the wind

you've been on the
still thawing piers in springtime
when the wind does the same thing
a gangbanger in a Chi Town jail does
after painting lipstick tits on a guy's back

all of a sudden you realize
twelve below zero is really fuckless cold
you haven't got your hair cut for a coon's age
you haven't shaved in about a week
you feel the cold numbing your hands

you never get used to relaxing
when you're still alone
after being alone
through another day's
twelve hour shift at the typer

and up here
in the Wisconsin woods
when it's twelve below zero
and your woman is sleeping alone
you can't stand being alone

you stay outside a little longer
and all that you accomplish
is thinking about your woman
and thinking about starting
another novel

you walk inside your place
you're still thinking about
your woman sleeping alone
it's really fuckless cold outside
your hands are totally numb

when you're alone at night
only your hands get cold
from twelve degrees below zero
only your hands tremble
from the fire down below

Ides of March sarong

the Ides of March came
and seemed to be conquering

fifty and sixty degree highs
for a tapestry of glorious days

stark murky gray sludgy harbor
enrapturing toward luscious blue

open shoreline shallows
clear of ice and starting to warm

seven pound starving prowling brown trout
hooked and landed alone with special net

still warm heart prepares rich
pink red fillets for others

gold bold morning sunrises
defeated by looming storm clouds

spring yearning grass again covered
with crisp linen morning frost

sole open expanse of again frigid harbor
battled by lone lifetime shoreline angler

special fishing boots dig into ice dappled
mother nature jagged harbor shoreline rocks

cold cunning wet barreling wind
making ice on eye guide tip of fishing rod

skin splits on casting and reeling knuckles
red droplets pumped through skin cracks

weary wild birds again stocking up
at weather beaten front yard bird feeder

chancing deer herds again stocking up
two lane state highway smattered by two carcasses

weather alerts again announce
another snowstorm is drawing near

lone lifetime shoreline angler
taking the fishing rod out of the truck

putting the fishing rod back in the garage
shifting the truck back into four wheel drive

pulling out of the driveway again empty
except for storm remnants still spiraling down

spring yearning grass
again nowhere to be seen

shrubs buds bulbs blossoms
again skirted by snow garment

lone lifetime shoreline angler
staring at March 29 on kitchen calendar

Ides of March sarong
Ides of March so wrong

spring yearning heart still pumping warm red
still cold harsh winter in northeastern Wisconsin

Front Porch Blues

the red Marlboro
is stale
the dead grass
is mud
the winter snow
is gone
the finest woman
is lonely

I remember the warmth
of the covers she pulled aside

I remember the warmth
of the comfort she wrapped

all around me
and best of all
all inside me

the red Marlboro
is stale
the dead grass
is mud
the finest woman
is lonely

I remember the peace
of everything I said being understood

I remember the peace
of unique desire meeting same old need

under those covers
and best of all
inside my heart

the red Marlboro
is stale
the winter snow
is gone
the finest woman
is lonely

Front Porch Blues still the same
I light up take the smoke down deep

Front Porch Blues still the same
searching for the strength one more time

inside my heart
oxygen of life
the hope

the yearning

my dictionary
tells me it is
a strong emotion of
longing or desire
especially
with tenderness

my dictionary
cannot convey to me
the yearning
in my heart
my head
my fingertips

my dictionary
could have kept it
a lot more
simple
and just called it
miserable

yearning
for her only her
the squirming nerves
the firecracker fuse making me
want to holler out for her
is way past longing

yearning
for her only her
the emptiness in my chest
as if my heart won't beat
the right way unless next to her
is way past desire

yearning
for her only her
the feel of her face in my hands
smell her hair kiss her forehead
listen to her breath deepen
is way past tenderness

the yearning is
the best part
the worst part
the hardest part
the truest part
all wrapped up into one

most grueling thing
a human being has to endure
I am certain of it
I laugh at marathon runners
and think of how easy they have it
as I yearn for her

Listen...

through the windows finally open
the birds of spring chirp and cackle
the neighbor drives by honking
the top finally down on his Mustang
all of those sounds swirling...

but I listen to the glide of her arm
gust of wind
I listen to the motion of her hand
rumble of thunder
I listen to her pointing finger
crack of lightning

nothing ever
so very loud
as the plus sign
on the pregnancy test...

Need the Rain?

for three days
and nights
the rain keeps
coming down

for three days
and nights
the sky keeps
looming glooming

maybe the fish
are biting
somewhere
right now

I promised
my beautiful
pregnantly hormonal woman
I won't go fishing in the rain

I don't want to
go fishing in the rain
I don't want to
go fishing at all

I don't want to
turn a page
in the good book
on the coffee table

I don't want to
go check my lottery ticket
and hear people at the store
say we need the rain

the only thing I feel like doing
is kissing my beautiful
pregnant woman
on the cheek neck lips

leading her upstairs
to her bed at her place
to slip under the covers
and forget about the rain

$9.84 an hour

forty hours per week
at the fine front desk
of the finest tourist resort
wasn't cutting it
with twin girls
due in January

so I took the $9.84 an hour
Friday night graveyard shift
at the gas station
with the convenience store
at the top of the hill
in this northeastern Wisconsin town

on the first night I worked
the local yocal gossip
was all about a crew
of big city thieves
passing through town
robbing all the gift shops

a couple weeks later
I got hit with a drive off at the pumps
and the manager informed me
I was responsible
for covering the drive off
out of my meager pay

a couple weeks after that
the sheriff came in right at dark
and told me I had just sold
a six pack of beer
to an undercover
sting operation officer

it took about a half hour
for the sheriff to explain it to me
the cash register kept beeping
for me to approve cash transactions
where the customer pays inside
if they don't decide to drive off

I told the sheriff that I hoped
he could understand I wasn't
being disrespectful
by not paying attention to him
but I was responsible for drive offs
and couldn't afford to be

the sheriff asked me if I needed
information on how to check IDs
and I told him no what I needed
were security cameras on the pumps
and security cameras inside the store
because I had to watch for inside thieves too

the sheriff said I would have to
appear in court before a judge
who would decide
if my fine would be
a minimum $350.00
or a maximum $550.00

I went home and found
ten stamps left on a roll
researched five new NYC literary agents
to query for representation of
my latest Chicago crime novel
and prepared my return response envelopes

the next morning I put
the queries in the mail
turned in my gas station shirt
and wondered if maybe
a NYC literary agent would like
a too small town crime novel

are you a...

I hopped out of my truck
in the Pamida parking lot
and I suppose I shouldn't
get too far without clarifying
a Pamida store is a
northern Wisconsin version
of a Walmart
okay
ahem

walking toward the store
the nasty November wind
lets me and the rest of the
poor bastards heading inside
know full damn well
why damn near everybody
leaves this too small tourist town
before the end of October
if they've got the money to leave

the wind is already too cold
but hey I'm feeling my oats
my painter writer artist lover woman
was kind to me earlier in the morning
and my fake hip doesn't hurt today
though the flu shot I got last month
didn't work against whatever I've got
but I'm fighting it strong I just need
some cold medicine

inside the store I find the cold pills
then I thoroughly enjoy
picking out a couple chocolate bars
for my woman who graciously
has me feeling my oats
as I walk up to the cash register
like a cock of the block
son of a big city gun
in this too small town

the cashier scans the cold pills
with her fancy schmancy wand
she picks up the chocolates as if
picking up dog turds from her lawn
she looks at me
and says
are you a senior
today is senior discount day
are you a senior, sir

I stare at the old cashier
she's got enough pancake
makeup on her face
to make a breakfast stack
all she needs is the milk and egg
all I need to do is say something
but no words come forth
until I manage to blurt out
NO, I am not a senior

walking back to my truck
I think about my twin daughters
two months away from their due date
inside my beautiful momma woman
and I think about all the
God forsaken years on the road
Chi Town Miami Los Angeles Louisville
until I finally landed way up here
in a writer's shack in the woods

forty three years old I put
the key in the truck ignition
and turn over the engine
thinking
if I can't peddle a novel
to New York City
I will be a senior
leading my daughters
out of this store

then I remember some
righteous editor dude
with an old fashioned poetry magazine
way the blessed hell over in England
linked on a newfangled website
with 43,000 hits per something
and this guy I don't know what
makes him feel his oats but he
just named me a 2009 top ten overseas poet

I pull away from the store
daydreaming
my twelve year old daughters
are eating the chocolates
I bought them inside
there is no employee
of the month or year or decade
photo of the old cashier
on the Pamida store wall

and I am a fifty five year old
senior father
smiling a wry smile
as my daughters
scrunch their noses
and look at me earnestly
after listening to me tell them
about a Pamida poem I wrote
twelve years ago

I stop my truck
outside the post office
still daydreaming
my twelve year old daughters
looking at the Pamida receipt
as I teach them the writer's benefit
from the Pamida senior discount
putting stamps on envelopes of poems
I let them put into the mailbox

The Sit-Down

after my prematurely contracting
pregnant lover woman
was unhooked from the monitors
the doc let us leave the hospital

before taking her home
to the ongoing bed rest she rues
we went on what became
an excursion at the local Walmart

I dropped her at the entrance
parked the 129,000 miles old truck
and walked toward her hoping
our twins stay inside her long enough

I expected to find her waiting for me
sitting in a wheelchair at the entrance
a regular reliable wheelchair as the world
has always known a wheelchair to be

I joined her in a standing position
the two of us staring in disbelief
at a humongous newfangled contraption
with a large sign affixed to the front

the sign declared the contraption to be
a Sit-Down Shopping System
and we proceeded to spend too much time
trying to get her into the thing

the Sit-Down Shopping System had
a large basket enclosure that we got open
and what looked to be two garbage can lid
hubcap dealies that concealed the front wheels

she managed to sit down without giving herself
a C-Section on the large basket enclosure
and I managed to start pushing her into the store
when the basket whipped open and the wheels locked

over came a rather unique human form
with the slithering pace of a salamander
otherwise known to mankind as
The Walmart Store Entrance Greeter

the greeter had a look on her face
as if she were greeting a recently
paroled multiple felony convict
now dating her only daughter

the greeter was squinting I think
it was hard to tell looking at her eyes
through her eyeglass lenses that looked
like broken soda bottles on a dirty beach

she told us that all we had to do
was lock the gate (the basket enclosure)
which she tried to do by banging it
like a toddler banging a toy on the floor

after my lover woman absorbed
the first couple basket enclosure bangings
against her pregnant belly
she blocked the greeter's banging with her hand

my lover woman told the greeter
she didn't want to deliver our babies
in the Walmart store entrance
and the greeter looked like she needed to fart

without further ado I figured out how to
safely ensconce my lover woman in the rig
and we finished our shopping
and headed on home

we sat down on the couch
she turned on the television
and a commercial was touting an all-day
Godfather Trilogy telecast on Thanksgiving

I went to bed thankful for those two American Heroes
I thought about Don Corleone and his son Michael
having their final sit-down near the Corleone garden
and then I began seeing things clearly

I thought about going back to Walmart
with my neighbor's deer hunting rifle
and visions of Walmart bringing back
the old wheelchair dancing in my head

What Matters Most

I was the guy who always said
I would be waiting downstairs in the lobby
or ready down on the street corner
waiting to pass out cigars

we were at the hospital in Green Bay
with the Neo Natal Intensive Care Unit
because my lover woman had preeclampsia
her blood pressure was 195 over 145

I was the guy who always said
I would be waiting downstairs in the lobby

and I was downstairs in the lobby
getting my lover woman admitted
after wondering if she was going to deliver
five weeks premature on the drive there

the docs said it would be too much
of a risk to my lover woman's life
if they didn't hurry up and induce labor
but the inducement took over 24 hours

I was the guy who always said
I would be ready on the street corner with cigars

I spent a long sleepless night
in a recliner next to the hospital bed
listening to my lover woman struggle
and falling deeper in love with her

in the morning the delivery doctor
took a long tubular device and
put it where no one but me
should be putting anything

I was the guy the nurses were reminding
to put on a surgical gown and cap

I expected a stark delivery room but
it looked like a big time Hollywood movie set
and I thought I was the only one watching
my lover woman struggling with her pain

a crew of nurses just for the delivery doctor
a bank of monitors along the far wall
a technician in front of each machine
all kinds of blinking and beeping

I thought I was the only one watching
my lover woman struggling with her pain

a full staff of doctors and assistants
incubators heart monitors lung monitors
and everything else the neo natal
intensive care team had with them

an anesthesiologist and his team
expecting a c-section delivery
on our Baby B lodged in a breech position
near my lover woman's ribs

the delivery doctor was telling his nurses
Baby A natural then Baby B by c-section

I kept watching my lover woman's
incredible focus and fortitude
falling even deeper in love with her
as she pushed with all her might

the delivery doctor said that Baby A
was lodged in the birth canal
and he was going to have to use
suction to get her delivered

*I was the guy who always said
I would be waiting downstairs in the lobby*

my lover woman kept pushing
and the delivery doctor kept suctioning
and finally Baby A came out with
one little peep of a cry

a neo natal ICU doctor put a mask
on Baby A's face and a nurse said
don't worry it's just to help her breathe
and what is this girl's name?

*her name is Amelia Elaine I said
then I looked at momma with awe and pride*

I watched with shock and worry
as the ICU team rubbed Amelia all over
like they were kneading dough
then tightened the mask on her face

Amelia wasn't moving at all
an ICU nurse said don't worry
she's exhausted from the stress
of being lodged in the birth canal

I was the guy who always said
I would be ready on the street corner with cigars

they weighed Amelia at five pounds
I looked over at beautiful momma
I saw the anesthesiologist and his team
getting ready for the impending c-section

I looked into beautiful momma's eyes
I watched her artist hands start to move
I knew what she was trying to do
I knew how I was going to help

the delivery doctor was backing away and
the anesthesiologist was putting on gloves

somehow someway I helped beautiful momma
focus her breathing and bear the pain
she worked her artisan hands until she had
repositioned Baby B for natural delivery

I could see the nurses' jaws dropping from
underneath their hospital masks
the doctors were shaking their heads in awe
and I was falling even deeper in love with momma

the delivery doctor hunkered back down and
I started thinking hey it's all down hill from here

it took beautiful momma only four minutes
to deliver our boldy crying Baby B
who kept swinging her arms like a prizefighter
as a nurse weighed her and asked for her name

Hannah Jane I said then I looked
at all the ICU doctors surrounding her
they weighed her at four pounds and
I bent down and Hannah smiled at me

I was the guy who always said
I would be waiting downstairs in the lobby

the ICU team had both babies cleaned up
and heading out in the incubators
the delivery doctor shook my hand
and the nurses all said congratulations

I got a couple nice pictures of both girls
I noticed a nurse calling in their vitals
to register their birth information
and finally I could smile with momma

I kissed beautiful momma and held her hand
feeling magnetized to her and loving the feeling

on our way out of the delivery room
the neo natal doctor stopped us and said
Baby B is healthy but I saw something in her
eyes and we're checking for Down Syndrome

all of a sudden the neo natal doctor was gone
and we were back in beautiful momma's room
waiting to ask the nurses just exactly
how long checking for Down Syndrome takes

Hannah looked me right in the eye and smiled
and the neo natal doctor saw Down Syndrome

there was nothing to prepare us
for being separated from our babies
and there was nothing to prepare us
for visiting our preemies in the ICU

Amelia and Hannah were so small
they made the incubators seem huge
and for too many long days and nights
we had to look at Hannah and wonder

I was the guy who always said
I would be ready on the street corner with cigars

I had gone home
to pack a bag for beautiful momma
the hospital was getting ready to release her
and the phone rang

never again do I ever want
to hear beautiful momma's voice
sound the way it did
when she told me yes it was Down Syndrome

I ended the phone call remembering how many times
I looked at Hannah in the incubator and thought no way

I folded up my cell phone and
sat on the edge of the bed
looking at all the bookshelves
custom built by beautiful momma

the bookshelves beautiful momma and I stared at
all throughout her pregnancy and bed rest
the bookshelves that we both said
felt so comforting to have all around the bedroom

it didn't take long and I wasn't surprised
my eyes focused on the Bukowski shelf
then my eyes settled on the title
that spoke to me and explained everything

What Matters Most
Is How Well You Walk Through The Fire

Circle of Life

nine months ago
the previous nine months
with the finest woman
seemed to be over

she had turned 39
I had turned 43
maybe we were just
too set in our own ways

she and I both had taken
the same old I.Q. test
way back when in the past
she had a 147 and I had a 145

nine months ago we were
both too smart for our own good
both too stubborn on our own
seemingly split apart

somehow someway we came
together the way true lovers do
she took me into her bedroom
she let her sexy nightie slip to the floor

nine months later I brought
an engagement ring out of my pocket
she smiled we cried tears of joy
she let me put the ring on her finger

tonight she is sleeping soundly
her sexy nightie tucked away in a drawer
she wore one of my big t-shirts
and my baggy pajama bottoms to bed

I am in the living room reading
by the light of our first Christmas tree
our newborn twin daughters are sleeping
for the moment

I am listening for stirring in baby cribs
and reading a posthumously released book
by a writer friend of mine
who died a year ago on Thanksgiving Day

the babies are sleeping soundlessly
and I am cursing myself again
for not making time to be better friends
with a helluva writer named Church

all of a sudden the babies are stirring
I set down the book and rush in silently
Momma left the connecting bedroom door open
but Momma really needs her sleep

I bend down to look into Hannah's crib
she winces then farts then maybe more
which makes her sister Amelia
chirp and fart and maybe more

two newborn twin sisters communicating in
stirring wincing chirping farting poop language
while Momma snores in the bedroom and I go
back to keeping alive a dead writer's words

The Lesson

our twin daughters are buckled
in their new high chairs
looking like they are ready
for an amusement park ride

I have come back from a spell
of banging on the typer
I sit down next to Beautiful Momma
as she feeds our baby girls

I lean and smell
Beautiful Momma's hair
the smell of her hair
enchanting me as always

I lean back and look at
her new wedding band
my eyes moist from knowing
she is proud that ring is on her finger

hands in my lap
I spin the wedding band on my finger
my eyes moist from feeling
how proud I am too

Beautiful Momma feeds Hannah and Amelia
until Amelia snatches the spoon
attempts to feed herself
then gags on the spoon

Beautiful Momma takes the spoon and says
let that be a lesson to you,
you can't put the spoon in so far,
Amelia, that's a lesson

Beautiful Momma once again starts
gently teaching our daughter
and my mind goes back to the
old neighborhood on the South Side of Chicago

I was closer to being a young boy
than being a teenager
and I was sitting out on the back stoop
with Uncle Ted on a Sunday afternoon

we were waiting for Uncle Ted's
last racing pigeon to finish the weekend race
by moving from the back alley telephone pole
to the confines of the pigeon coop

once all the pigeons were inside the coop
Uncle Ted could use the clocking device
to stamp the time of day on the bands
clamped around their legs

the finishing time of the last bird
had much to do with the ultimate
gambling payoff to the winning owner
so it was a particularly quiet time on the stoop

all of a sudden the husband next door
started yelling at the wife next door
their kitchen window was open
and their kids spilled out into the backyard

all of that commotion sent the last pigeon
fluttering away instead of into the coop
and Uncle Ted pointed at me with his
jagged stump of an index finger

Uncle Ted said
let that be a lesson to you,
for when you have
kids of your own someday,

you unnerstan' me, Robert?
you do like your father does
you always let your kids see
how much you love their mother

back then
the last thing on my mind
was having kids of my own
someday

but after Uncle Ted spoke those words
I spent the rest of my life paying attention
to how my father always showed everybody
how much he loved my mother

and I've grown up to finally
have kids of my own someday
and it's the most natural feeling in the world
to show everybody how much I love their mother

it's a lesson I'm sure I would have
come to understand on my own
growing up and watching my father
but Uncle Ted made me understand much sooner

I'm thankful
as I watch
my wife
feed our daughters

thankful for
my wife
thankful for
our daughters

thankful for the memory
of Uncle Ted's lesson
thankful for all the lessons
from watching my father

poems in her head

there was a time
before my wife was my wife
three decades of time actually
when she was a
very prolific writer

except the people
closest to her
couldn't understand her
and misconstrued her and despised her
for being a writer

so she learned to keep her writing hidden
rather than be scorned for it
until she was living through far too many years
separated from actively considering
that indeed she was a writer

on the blessed night we first met
I happened to be just back in town
after a book tour in London and San Francisco
for the Kerouac anthology I co-edited and wrote for
and Joie said to me *what do you do?*

I told her *I am a writer*
she shrugged and sighed and said *well aren't we all*
so without missing a beat I asked her
where she sent her stuff
and she said *nowhere*

after we met that night
it didn't take too long for us to be together
and out into the open
like glorious rainfall to a drought crop
came all of her writing

then came her new writing
and all of a sudden no doubt about it
she was shaping and crafting poems
and polishing them like what they were
fine gems

it took me quite a while to convince her
then she sent poems to a couple publications
and without ever knowing
about rejection slips
she was a published and paid poet

then came difficult pregnancy and
premature births and twins in all their needy glory
and this morning in the midst of feeding the girls
during a stand up breakfast of grapefruit in the kitchen
she says to me

I'm still writing poems in my head
I don't know when I'll have the time
to put them down on paper
but I am still
writing poems in my head

and so will come a time
when her poems are all on paper again
and then kind readers put your money down
on the book that says *Poems by Joie Powell*
for that book shall be a winner

Author's Acknowledgement

The author gratefully acknowledges the following publications that originally published the noted poems in this book:

THE MOON—The Publication for Writing and Art (Fort Wayne, Indiana): Global Warning, American Spirit, Solitaire, Normal..., Hey Ma, survival of the fittest, new economy of scale, stiff upper lip, just another normal human being, Bipartisan, the yearning, Need the Rain?, $9.84 an hour, The Sit-Down

STREETZINE (Louisville, Kentucky): Bored on the Fourth of July, 2008

THE BEATLICK NEWS (Santa Fe, New Mexico): Woman and Man

ALT-CURRENT PRESS (Cambridge, Massachusetts): when the pen is the needle and the paper is the spoon

BEAT SUPER NOVA RASA (Venezia, Italy): forever sordid shame

THE DIRTY GOAT (New York, New York): only your hands tremble

SAGE TRAIL MAGAZINE (Santa Barbara, California): Front Porch Blues, only the serious know

ASKEW POETRY JOURNAL (Ventura, California): Listen...

PURPLE PATCH (West Bromwich, England): are you a...

About the Author

Robert M. Zoschke was born in Oak Park, Illinois, in 1965. Until 1993 he lived in and around Chicago, where he was an award-winning advertising copywriter and a winner of a Chicago Sun-Times essay contest before taking to the road. After living in Miami, Los Angeles, and Louisville, he took to the woods of Wisconsin to finish writing his first novel, *A Gangster's Promise*, registered with the Writer's Guild and excerpted in the anthology *Other Voices* from Wisconsin's Cross+Roads Press.

In 2007, he co-edited and wrote for the international tribute anthology *Reflections Upon the 50th Anniversary of Jack Kerouac's On the Road* (Published in Heaven Books, Louisville, Kentucky). In 2008, his book *Door County Blues* was released (Published in Heaven Books). *Door County Blues*—a collection of his short stories, poems, essays, letters, and newspaper parodies—was recognized as a # 1 bestseller in 2008 in Door County, Wisconsin. In 2009, England's Purple Patch Poetry Magazine named him a Top Ten Overseas Poet.

He currently resides with his wife Joie and their four children in a deer-proof writer's commune nestled into the woods of far northeastern Wisconsin.